AF778209

Table of Contents

Dedicated to the following

All investors, me included, are forever indebted to the following authors and scholars for their roles in contributing to our knowledge of the market and teaching us how to invest. Here are the names of these distinguished gentlemen and scholars.

Charles Ellis, Rex Sinquefield, Roger Ibbotson, Harry Markowitz, William Sharpe, William Bernstein, Richard Ferri, Larry Swedroe, W. Scott Simon, Frank Armstrong, and John C. Bogle.

Technical editors: Jerry Buchheit, Craig Arola, Thomas Wang and The Vanguard Group.

To those who organized and manage our website at www.morningstar.com: Taylor Larimore and Mel Lindauer—two great and very sharp guys who post thoughtful answers to our questions. The Diehard's site has had over 375,000 postings to date.

Thanks to Leonora Schaelling who edited this book.

And to the man who created the most valuable tool for the individual investor ever conceived, who has generously given of his time and energy for the small investor, who is the champion of all who have been successful in their investment programs due to his foresight and endless energy, the man who we all cherish, our leader and mentor John C. Bogle, Founder of The Vanguard Group, Inc. and Vanguard Funds.

We call ourselves Diehards, a group of dedicated investors who follow the strategy outlined in this book. We readily share our expertise to those investors who need our help.

Introduction

Congratulations! By sheer chance, you have found a book that will show you how to make money in the stock market. By following these directions, you will succeed in building a nest egg to enjoy your retirement years in comfort. I am going to lay out a specific set of plans that are easy to follow. As a rule of thumb, retirement income should be at least 70%–80% or more of your income just prior to retirement. Together, we will establish the required monthly additions to your investment account to meet this objective.

Some of the plans require your periodic attention annually to rebalance your portfolio to control risk while other plans attend to these details without your participation whatsoever. We will be using techniques endorsed and recommended by some of the finest minds and students of the stock market and supported by rigorous academic studies. The plans offered have been constructed using Modern Portfolio Theory (MPT), which provides the backbone of all rational investment strategies. We will not be selecting individual securities as often recommended by Wall Street brokers; such activities most often lack a cohesive strategy and result in returns empirical evidence show are sub-optimum. Selecting an individual security based on prior performance is like selecting a line to stand in at a super market: the moment you jump in one line, it stops moving.

It may come as a surprise, but determining which funds to purchase for your portfolio will be the easiest part of the program. The hard part of the plan is sticking with the program. To assist in this required task, I have supplied you with a wealth of information to convince you of the merits of the plan. You will be in touch with your peers who will advise and council you as required through a website I will provide. You will also be able to attend periodic meetings with fellow investors at select locations throughout the country.

We will be using our computers to keep our investment plan up to date, to monitor our progress, and to obtain advice from our fellow investors who follow similar investment strategies. We will be using no-load index funds in a manner consistent with Modern Portfolio Theory.

Indexing the stock market makes a lot of sense for four reasons.

- Index funds have low expense ratios.
- They perform better than almost all active strategies.
- They reduce the desire to chase hot funds since you already own the stocks that are performing well.
- They are tax efficient. By tax efficient, I'm referring to strategies that minimize taxable events thus siphoning off funds from your investment that could have remained in the account and continued to compound until withdrawal at retirement time. (Adapted from the book *Common Sense on Mutual Funds* by John C. Bogle, a must read for every investor.)

We are going to talk a lot about tax efficiency because avoiding taxable events can lead to an increase of as much as 30% to 50% in the final value of your portfolio at retirement time. How do we minimize taxes? To the extent possible, we put our investments in tax-deferred or tax-free accounts such as a 401(k), a regular IRA, or Roth IRA. We reduce our transactions to a minimum by not trading for our own account or purchasing mutual funds that trade constantly. For a good discussion on how to title your account, see Chapter 7 of Richard Ferri's book *Protecting*

Your Wealth in Good Times and Bad. On average, actively managed mutual funds turn over their portfolios every 15 months. New regulations now require mutual funds to report to the shareholder the effects of taxes caused by portfolio turnover. The average investor is generally unaware of the magnitude of the dilution of portfolio value by tax payments that could have been avoided with a buy-and-hold strategy.

Some of you will have already purchased securities; they will be integrated into the program as required. Specifically, we will be selling substantially all individually owned stocks and actively managed mutual funds in such a manner as to match those with gains to those held at a loss and investing the proceeds in index mutual funds. We will be transferring your individual securities to a deep-discount online broker whose commissions are as much as 88% lower than some full-service brokers. Selling off securities with losses against portfolio taxable gains is called tax harvesting.

Some of you may be in the position of having started saving too late for your retirement. For you, I will have specific suggestions to attempt to recover lost ground. This will involve tilting your portfolio allocation towards asset classes with higher expected returns (e.g., toward Small-Cap index funds and value funds that capture the value premium). Such a strategy comes with higher risk and higher expected returns that depend on the market to continue rewarding the investor as it has done in the past for taking these added risks.

By combining equities with fixed income index funds we can iron out fluctuations in the value of the portfolio as a whole. As you approach retirement we want to be in a position where sharp declines in stocks will not impair your savings—a fancy way of saying we don't want to run out of money.

The Author

At this point, it is perhaps a good time to tell you something about me. I was born in 1927 and was the eldest of four children. Dad was a stock market speculator well known in financial circles in Southern California. My Dad never played catch with me; the family never went camping or to the beach with Dad. But during my summer vacations, Dad and I would visit broker offices, conduct research, talk with brokers, and watch market prices. He traded stocks every day the market was open using a system he had devised. On weekends, we would study the annual reports of various companies as well as Value Line reports and chart market prices. By the age of seven, I could chart, read Standard & Poor's (S&P) reports, and read the ticker tape. I even had my favorite stocks.

At Claremont Men's College, I took an MBA-style course with an emphasis in economics, corporate finance, and tax law. After college, I worked in accounting, finance, and capital budgeting at a number of large corporations such as U.S. Steel, U.S. Borax & Chemical, Rhodes Corporation, Gulf Oil, and Litton Industries. On some of these jobs, I was stationed overseas in Europe and South America. For a time, I worked with the people on staff with Aristotle Onasis on international projects. In 1970, I purchased a minority shareholder interest in a small public company traded in the over-the-counter market called Jensen Industries.

At Jensen, I was the Chief Financial Officer in charge of all financial matters, doing mergers and acquisition work, secondary stock issues, and tender offers in addition to my duties as Chief Financial Officer. As a member of the

Board of Directors, I was responsible to the shareholders in a fiduciary capacity.

I filed the required disclosures with the Securities Exchange Commission (SEC) to issue additional shares of the company's stock, wrote proxy statements, and represented the company at stock analyst meetings. I applied for and obtained a listing for the company on the American Stock Exchange (AMEX).

Today, I am an investor with substantial holdings, fully retired and living solely off my portfolio income and a little social security. I also teach Modern Portfolio Theory at the local community college and keep up to date on new strategies and investment techniques. I use the strategies illustrated herein. I hold in excess of 8,200 stocks and bonds in my portfolio all in index and exchange traded funds.

Most investors spend far too many hours reading what I call financial pornography in the financial media. This leads to both unwise trading decisions and continuous trading of stocks into and out of their portfolios. Most investors end up then with a portfolio with a mish mash of individual stocks and mutual funds. Their portfolios have been constructed without a solid plan. As a result, their portfolios exhibit levels of risk well above the market risk. An index investor knows when he takes on risk that he does so with the understanding that it is very likely that, over time he can expect to achieve the expected returns that taking additional risk promises to provide.

Bet your full-service broker never discussed these things with you. I bet other investment books you may have read have not pointed out the risk factors and how you can control the level of risk of your portfolio.

Facts about Investing in Stocks and Bonds

The focus of this book will be on the use of index mutual funds and Exchange Traded Funds (ETFs). To understand how an index fund works, you must know about indexes. Charles Dow created the first index in 1896. It measured 12 stocks traded on the New York Stock Exchange. The closing prices of these 12 stocks were added up, divided by 12, and published in a tip sheet now known as the *Wall Street Journal*. Today, the Dow Jones Industrial Average consists of 30 stocks adjusted for the stock splits, stock dividends, mergers, and other events that have occurred over the years so as to maintain the historical continuity of the index. It is a price-weighted index—a smaller company has as much influence on the index as a much larger one. The index has more historical value than usefulness as an index for a portfolio strategy.

Modern indexes are market value weighted. A stock with a higher total market value will have more influence in the index than a stock with lower market value. Most market value indexes use shares issued and outstanding multiplied by the current price (total market value) to determine its weight in the index. In other words, companies with higher market value will have a greater influence on the index. Indexes are used to measure the performance of funds and their managers. They are also used to construct mutual funds that match the performance of an index, known as index mutual funds. There are about 500 stock indexes representing, for example, small companies (small-cap), large companies (large-cap), foreign securities, and the total stock market; others only measure sectors of the market such as basic industries, retail, finance companies, and foreign securities. There are about 40 bond indexes representing corporate bonds, municipal bonds, and treasury bonds. These indexes are also market value weighted.

When you buy an index fund, you are called a passive investor. You do not try to outguess other investors or "professional fund managers." The reason is simple: when you buy an index fund for your portfolio, you will outperform after taxes and over time the majority of the best professional fund managers. The compelling argument for index funds is that the compounding of cost savings, the law of averages, and the passage of time are all working in concert for you year after year. Importantly, they defy human intervention-yours or the professional-and continue to work in your behalf whether you're paying attention or not. I have heard the saying, "Why look for the needle in the haystack" referring to the process of selecting stocks, "just buy the entire haystack." You will be amazed how many individual securities you can own with an investment of only $1,000 using an index fund.

In the early 1970s, Charles Ellis evaluated the performance of a number of large pension funds and found that they underperformed the S&P 500 index. Charley coined the term "a loser's game" to describe the efforts of those who devote extraordinary effort trying to beat the consensus of all other investors in the market. **Scads of highly sophisticated follow-up studies have verified this fact**. Uninformed investors have a great difficulty understanding how a simple basket of securities, which contains good and bad companies, profitable and losing companies, can out-perform a portfolio of individual securities selected by a staff of highly skilled stock market analysts. I recommend you buy and read Charley's book titled *Winning the Loser's Game* by Charles D. Ellis

Wall Street brokerage houses sell the public on the idea that research can uncover stocks that will outperform the market as a whole. **Facts shoot down this assumption. By way of example, as of September 2001, the recommendations of the 12 major brokerage firms with five-year performance records averaged a total cumulative return of 29.6% compared to 62.7% for the S&P 500 index.**

In the recommended reading list, I also suggest that you read the book by W. Scott Simon titled *Index Mutual Funds- Profiting from an Investment Revolution.* I quote from the preface written by John C. Bogle "The simple case for index funds is part theory, part practice, and part arithmetic. Theory says that since (a) gross returns earned by investors as a group must equal the gross returns earned by the total stock market, (b) net returns—after advisory fees and other investment expenses—earned by investors as a group must fall short of the returns of the market by these costs. Index funds have costs and expenses far lower than actively managed funds and, therefore, produce superior returns."

Returns earned by the average equity actively managed mutual fund in the past, have typically fallen short of the returns of the appropriate stock market index by an amount approximately equal to the operating cost expenses and transaction costs incurred by the funds. In fact, only 25% of actively managed equity funds have outpaced the appropriate index, and no one has ever suggested a methodology by which those few winners could have been selected in advance.

To the novice investor, a skilled broker can easily convince you that their staff of experts can select for you a superior portfolio of stocks or an actively managed mutual fund that will outperform an index fund. I'm going to be blunt. Despite all that you have read in the financial press, most people should not attempt to invest in individual securities with their serious money. Why? It's too risky. Investing is all about risk and expected return. If you are going to take a risk, it is imperative that you achieve a commensurate return. To balance the risk and return for a portfolio of individual securities requires a portfolio of approximately $1,000,000 to achieve proper diversification and to match market risk. Invest in one index mutual or an Exchange Traded Fund to achieve the same results. Today, we have index mutual funds and Exchange Traded Funds (ETFs) that track various indexes. These funds provide adequate diversification to ensure that the returns match market risk for their respective asset classes. If you read the recommended book written by John C. Bogle you will appreciate the importance of keeping investment expenses as low as possible. Perhaps we should, at this point, compare the costs of running an actively managed fund with the costs incurred by an index fund. A couple aged 50 and above must plan for at least 30 years of retirement, thus I show you the effects of fund expenses and taxes for an actively managed fund and an exchange traded mutual fund. Front-end load is not included in these numbers.

Comparison Based on Current Expenses for a One-time Investment of $100,000 Held for 30 Years

	Average Actively Managed Fund	Total Market Index Fund (VTI)
Total Return	8.00%	8.00%
Transaction Costs	1.00%	0.15%
Expense Ratio	1.50%	0.07%
Income Taxes	1.90%	0.28%
Total Cost	4.40%	0.50%
Net Return	3.60%	7.50%

Here I show you the cumulative effects of costs and taxes in terms of dollars and cents over a thirty-year period.

Few investors are aware of how deferring taxes and using low cost funds add to terminal portfolio values. The average actively managed fund incurs approximately 30% more risk than the total market risk as measured by the total market index shown in the chart. One should not take on additional risk without the promise of additional return. This is just common sense. There are tons of studies backing up this statement.

After 30 years	Average Actively Managed Fund	Total Market Index Fund (VTI)
Total Return	$1,006,266	$1,006,266
Transaction Costs	$163,031	$39,231
Expense Ratio	$244,546	$18,308
Income Taxes	$309,759	$73,231
Total Cost	$717,336	$130,770
Net Return	$288,930	$875,496

Transaction fees include broker commissions, the bid/ask spread (the brokers profit for entering into the transaction), and impact costs (actively managed portfolios turn their portfolios every 15 months on average). Most index funds trade very little, just enough to track their respective indexes. The expense ratio of actively managed funds averages 1.5% of assets under management compared to as low as 0.07% for a total market exchange traded fund. It is the high turnover of actively managed funds that causes these taxable events, reducing return by 1.9 % from the effects of income taxes.

The significance of the difference in returns between an index fund and the average actively managed mutual fund is amazing. The impact of income taxes and higher expenses over your accumulation phase over 30 years is a difference of three times in end portfolio values. The average investor just does not realize that every dollar paid out in expenses and taxes is lost forever and that if these sums had been retained in the portfolio, the compound effect over time is enormous, as shown in the exhibit above.

In this example we used a total stock market fund that is extremely tax efficient. Other index asset classes (small-cap and the value class) are not as tax efficient but as a general rule, less tax efficient asset classes should be held in a tax-deferred account. If, however you rebalance annually you will garner a bonus return of an additional 1% more or less.

Over the next 20 years, many highly qualified economists, including Nobel Prize winners, estimate that market returns will be in the range of 7% to 8%—far less than in the previous 20 years. Since active mutual fund's costs average 4.4%, we can expect active funds to return somewhere around 3.6%, giving a minuscule return after factoring in 3%–3.5% inflation. The twenty-year forecast was made using Gordon's formula, a method of forecasting future returns that has withstood the test of time.

Yes, there are successful actively managed mutual funds that, in any one year, or for a string of years, have outperformed index funds. To date, no one has figured out how to locate these winners before the fact, and studies have shown that this year's hot funds have a tendency to disappear from the hot list the following year.

Brokers who sell actively managed mutual funds usually charge a front-end load. Back-end load funds are the broker's darling—the fees are actually higher. Caution: if you are the target of a mutual fund presentation, beware that new mutual funds right out of the incubator will show fantastic performance. That is easy. Just start 20 funds and after a year or so, pick the best one and sell it to the public. Is this fraud? No. It is legal but not very nice. Never buy any actively managed fund that does not have a Morningstar rating. Morningstar only rates funds that have been existence for three years or more.

Did you know a stockbroker does not even need to have a high school diploma and does not necessarily know anything about finance; they are just nice people who know how to sell. With the right incentive, your stockbroker can and will sell you anything. Inquire about a specific security or a product or an industry and he will sell you the stock. That is what brokers are good at doing—it just happens they sell securities. If they can't capture 2% of your portfolio value every year, it is likely they will be looking for another job because their desk and phone will go to someone who can get that 2%. As you have seen, a little 2% each and every year of your investing horizon can add up to a whopping 30%–50% decrease in the end value of your portfolio at retirement.

The typical broker has about 200 active accounts with an average portfolio market value of $75,000 each that will generate $300,000 in annual commissions ($75,000 X 200 X 2%). He keeps one third, and his employer gets the balance.

He is constantly searching for new clients. How much time do you think he has to work on your account? I never met a broker I didn't like; they are really nice fellows and can talk stocks with an air of expertise and authority. They know about companies you have never heard of manufacturing exciting new products that promise extraordinary profits. When you use a proven index fund strategy, you know nothing about the companies that you invest in. You don't care. What you do know is that you are following a strategy that will, on balance, and over time, yield superior results, better than your peers, outperform 90% of broker-recommended portfolios, and avoid taxable events to the extent possible until your retirement years when you start withdrawing funds with embedded tax liabilities. The beauty of a Roth IRA is that all of the capital gains, dividends and interest income that have accumulated in the Roth can be withdrawn tax-free.

We are going to use index funds as our investment vehicle. As I mentioned, an index fund is a mutual fund that tracks an index, which is a basket of securities that corresponds to a precise definition of the contents. You are going to be in very select company with your investment strategy. Here are some of the large public employee pension plans that are using the strategy you will be following:

- Washington State—100% of assets indexed
- California—85% of assets indexed
- Florida—67% of assets indexed
- New York—75% of assets indexed
- Connecticut—84% of assets indexed

*Adapted from The Lazy Person's Guide to Investing by Paul B. Farrell Ph.D.

To conclude, there are mountains of theoretical evidence and empirical studies that show a strategy of employing no-load index funds provides superior returns with less risk than actively managed portfolios of individual securities or aggressively managed mutual funds.

Experienced investors know and have experienced the violent fluctuations in stock prices as the outlook for the fortunes of individual companies and even entire business sectors change over time. There are some people who think they can forecast the economy and its effect on the market price of individual securities or sectors of the economy. Empirical evidence collected over the last 35 years has proven these notions incorrect. I, along with other academics, challenge the assertions of these people and offer proof that no one can successfully select individual securities and outperform the market that reflects the wisdom of all of the investors participating in the market. We maintain and offer proof that no one can successfully time the market—that is, forecast when stock prices will increase or decline in advance of the event—or even pick stocks that the market has under or overvalued. What this means is that all of the research by those very clever, dedicated stock analysts working on Wall Street all producing research reports that are interesting reading but worthless paper and of no value to the individual investor.

Ninety percent of individual investors purchase individual securities based on broker recommendation or what they read or hear from the media or purchase actively managed mutual funds sold by their brokers. It is of interest to see how these individuals faired during the recent bull market.

I quote from the report titled "Quantitative Analysis of Investor Behavior" by Dalbar Associates, the 2003 update of a study paid for by the mutual fund industry. "Most individuals are unable to profitably invest in the market and are left with equity returns lower than inflation. **The average equity fund investor earned a paltry 2.57% annually compared to inflation of 3.14% and the 12.2% the S&P 500 index returned for the last 19 years (1984–2003).**"

The Dalbar study has some flaws that under-states the performance of the average investor. A reasonable estimate of investor performance is 4% to 8% below the S&P performance for the period. Therefore, I estimate that the average investor returned from 4.2% to 8.2% for the period compared to the S&P index (12.2%) for the last 19 years.

The period covered by the Dalbar report was the greatest bull market in history. The point is that the average investor has been misled by the financial community that their experts can assist you in beating market returns. History shows that the financial advice of full-service brokers and their analysts is worthless.

One of the problems facing the investor who is saving for retirement is the fact that inflation of the dollar over time takes a terrible toll of his savings. One keeps a minimum of 30% equities in his portfolio because historically stocks have traditionally, but not always, produced returns in excess of inflation. Another method to hedge against inflation is to purchase Treasury Inflation Protected Securities (TIPS). Vanguard has a fund that holds TIPS, whose symbol is VIPSX. Go to the Vanguard site and read up on TIPS.

Foreign equities are good diversifiers and will reduce portfolio risk. They may also provide a hedge against inflation of the dollar as well. The stocks of foreign countries experience, at times, economic conditions that differ in direction and magnitude from our economy As a consequence, the prices of foreign securities tend to diverge from the prices of our domestic stocks. The technical term to measure this divergence is called the coefficient of correlation.

By way of example, the Swiss Franc cost the U.S. tourist in the 1950's about a quarter. Today the Swiss Franc costs 50 cents. Our Federal Reserve System controls and manipulates our currency. They seem happy if the dollar depreciates by a 3% to 3.5% each year. I graduated from college in 1951, and the first dollar I earned out of school is worth only 13 cents today.

Exchange Traded Funds

Exchange Traded Funds (ETFs) are one of the most exciting and innovative products to appear since the mutual fund. An ETF share represents ownership designed to correspond to a portfolio of underlying securities either the broad market or industry sectors of the market, segments of the broad market such as large-cap, small-cap, value, and growth segments; or international markets. Most ETFs combine the features of an open-end mutual fund and a stock. ETFs trade on exchanges just like stocks. Most ETFs are designed to track market indexes. For the year ended 2004, the ETFs managed by iShares were tax efficient and did not distribute any capital gains.

ETFs allow the investor to buy and sell an entire portfolio of stocks in a single transaction. This allows the investor instant diversification within a single security. Most ETFs track an index and permit the use of passive investment techniques. A few ETFs track bond indexes.

ETFs are like mutual funds, but they trade on the exchanges all day just like stocks. There are certain advantages in constructing a portfolio of ETFs. The mechanism of creating the portfolio of stocks embedded in the ETF is too complicated to describe here and not necessary to our objective. Suffice it to say, the actions of other fund shareholders cannot cause a taxable event in your portfolio. Also, the expenses are typically very low and competitive with some no-load index mutual funds. If you are a small investor use **MB-TRADING.** They charge a $1.00 per transaction minimum commission.. Some experts forecast the day when ETFs will replace mutual funds. I will present for your approval portfolios using ETFs.

Bonds

The Vanguard Group has a larger selection of bond funds than any other mutual fund company. Bonds are used in portfolios to control risk. They are the best diversifier of all the asset classes. You will note that I use bonds in each of the model portfolios. Here is a description of some of the Vanguard bond funds. Check the Vanguard website for current returns and durations.

Symbol	Description	Duration (yrs)	Yield
VMLTX	LMT-TERM TAX EXEMPT	*	*
VBISX	SHORT TERM BOND INDEX	*	*
VSGBX	SHORT-TERM FEDERAL	*	*
VWSTX	SHORT-TERM TAX EXEMPT	*	*
VFISX	SHORT-TERM TREASURY	*	*
VWEHX	HIGH-YIELD CORPORATE	*	*
VBIIX	INTERMEDIATE TERM BOND INDEX	*	*
VWITX	INTER-TERM TAX EXEMPT	*	*
VFITX	INTER-TERM TREASURIES	*	*
VFSTX	SHORT-TERM INVESTMENT GRADE	*	*

*Obtain current information from the Vanguard web site.

The theoretical basis of portfolio design was established by Harry Markowitz in the 1950s when he showed how a portfolio of stocks and bonds reduces portfolio risk and he developed the mathematical formulas to allocate the weight among asset classes. As a rule of thumb, the lower the correlation between asset classes, the better they are as a portfolio diversifier and thus reduce portfolio risk.

Bonds with longer maturities have higher rates of interest. The bonds in the each of the above asset classes have associated with each class a term called duration. Interest rates are set by the market. A complicated mathematical formula calculates the duration of a single bond or a portfolio of bonds that accounts for the all cash flows in terms of their present value. The duration of a bond portfolio tells us how far the market price a bond portfolio will rise or fall with a 1% change in the market rate of interest. By way of example, a bond portfolio with duration of two years will decrease in market value by 2% if the market interest rate increases by 1%. A bond portfolio with duration of six years will fluctuate 6% in value with a 1% change in the market rate of interest.

As stated above we use bonds and bond index funds to adjust portfolios to meet your volatility and risk tolerance. During your retirement period you do not want to be cashing in your stocks during a period when stock prices have fallen. To do so puts you at risk of running out of money and we don't like that do we? On the other hand a portfolio that is too conservative puts us at risk of having our nest egg eaten up by inflation. I recommend as a rule of thumb that annually you adjust your portfolio allocation where you keep the bond portion equal to your age.

Thus when stock prices are low you will be drawing funds from the bond portion of your portfolio rather than cashing in your equity index funds.

For the majority of individual investors, I recommend buying bond funds over purchasing individual issues.

Bonds can, and do at times, default and become worthless; a portfolio of bonds mitigates the magnitude of this risk.

Your Brokerage Account

If you have earned income from wages and salaries, open a Roth IRA account with The Vanguard Group, Inc. and contribute the maximum allowable funds yearly to the account. All the money that the Roth IRA earns is tax-free. A couple aged 50 and over can put $9,000 into their Roth account even if only one has earned income. You see your spouse can have a Roth IRA as well even if she has little or no earned income. The amount a husband and wife can sock away goes up to $10,000 in 2006 and 2007 and up to $12,000 in 2008. A Roth IRA is the best thing going tax-free accumulation and no tax at withdrawal of funds from the account.

Personally, I would use Vanguard for my Roth IRA. Set up with your bank to remit a minimum of $50.00 to the account each month. Start the account with $1,000. All income and capital gains in a Roth IRA are tax free, unlike a regular IRA where all income and capital gains are taxable at regular tax rates when withdrawn. You should contact a qualified tax advisor on setting up tax-free and tax-deferred accounts. I am a firm believer that an investor should prepare his own tax return. The proper management of your investments to follow the letter of the law is extremely important. You must take advantage of the tax incentives offered the investor prior to the end of the tax year. Going to a tax advisor to have your return prepared is too late to maximize after tax profits. J.K.Lasser sells and excellent book to enable you to prepare your return. Like everything the government does, there are all kinds of restrictions on the amounts you can put into these accounts and who qualifies.

The funds in the regular IRA will accumulate tax-free during the period that you are contributing, but all of the balance comes out at regular income tax rates when you start withdrawing. That means that the account converts what should have been a capital gain and taxed at lower rates to ordinary income taxed at higher rates. It's your call, but I would personally rather purchase what is called tax-managed index funds and hold them in a Vanguard account than use a regular IRA.

For investors who have securities with a full-service broker, I want you to do the following: get out all of the trading slips that you can find and add up the commission charges and any other fees including mutual fund loads, front-end loads, and back-end loads. Now multiply the number of slips by $5.00 (the commission for the broker I'm about to recommend). Subtract this total from commission charges and fees. The result is the money you have wasted dealing with a full-service broker. Simply put, there is no product offered by any full-service broker that belongs in your portfolio—without exception. **If you don't believe me, do yourself a favor and read the book in the recommended list by that fellow Simon.**

Now here is what you do with your present portfolio: transfer the whole portfolio to Brown Co . recently merged with E-Trade. Call them up and ask for an account transfer form and follow the instructions. Trades when necessary will cost you $5.00 each. There are two good reasons I selected this broker for you. First, the low, low commission, and second, you can remain fully invested at all times

For the small investor consider **MB-TRADING** commissions are one cent per share with a $1.00 minimum per transaction. An account can be opened for $2,000. To open a margin account requires $5,000. They require $25,000 in the account if you are thinking of day trading.

Just don't try day trading unless you have a deep need to loose money. The same observation holds for those of you who are thinking of speculating with commodity futures.

As of December 1, 2005 ETRADE purchased Brown Co. I was advised that the commission structure would not change for the first 5,000 shares traded in a day of a single security.

"Unfortunately, proper investing principles are not taught to the general public. There are no required courses on investing in high school or trade schools, and investing is not a part of the standard curriculum at colleges, law schools or medical schools. Generally, when it comes to financial education, most people are self-taught usually through expensive trial and error." *All about Asset Allocation* by Richard A. Ferri.

My little book contains all you really need to know about investing. Just pick out a model portfolio and start investing on a regular basis. Expect that your portfolio will at times have a huge loss at times. Such losses are normal and will occur from time to time. We Diehards have a saying "stay the course". Log on to the web site www.morningstar.com and post your feelings to the group. As I write there is a one-time $5.00 registration fee to post questions or state your views on his site. I would urge you to pay the one time fee and make use of this valuable resource. Many of our highly talented authors visit this web site on a daily basis others less often. Browsing the site is always free.

An Investment Program for the Young Investor

If you can't establish the discipline to live on less than you earn, then no amount of investment advice will help. I suggest you read the book titled *The Richest Man in Babylon by George S.* Clason This classic on personal finance has helped millions, and it will help you, too. Together, we are going to build a portfolio for you. We are going to begin with a very simple portfolio to get you started, and let you experience the ups and downs of the market first hand. It is one thing to say, "I understand that the market is volatile, and I can take the risk" and quite another to experience volatility first hand with real money-your money.

We are going to earn the market rate of return on your investment portfolio. This in and of itself will be a huge accomplishment-something realized by only 10% of individual investors.

If you had told a Wall Street executive 50 years ago that an individual investor could purchase a slice of the stock in 3,500 companies without paying a commission, he would have fainted dead away, woke up, and jumped out of his Wall Street penthouse window.

Well, Mr. Wall Street Executive, get ready to jump. We are going to buy an index mutual fund from The Vanguard Group that tracks the entire U.S. stock market, all 7,500 stocks of publicly traded securities in the U.S. market. A little about Vanguard. The company was founded by John C. Bogle back in 1976 and today, is the largest no-load mutual fund company in the United States with $800 billion in assets under management and some 19,300,000 shareholders. Yes, the investors own the company. When you buy a Vanguard fund, you become an owner in the company. Any profit made by the company after costs are returned to you in the form of reduced fees. That is what a mutual company is. Every year, you will get a proxy statement asking you to vote on important matters and for members of the board of directors. There is no full-service brokerage company that will sell you a share of any fund managed by Vanguard. Some of the largest pension funds and trusts purchase funds from Vanguard at fees very similar to those you will pay.

Why are we buying a sample of all of the securities traded in the market? There is a ton of evidence that shows it is extremely difficult to obtain, without taking more risk, returns in excess of the market return. If someone asks you what stocks you own, just say all of them. Selecting individual securities is as difficult as looking for a needle in a haystack. Remember, why look for the needle in the haystack? Just buy the entire haystack!

At this point, please accept the fact that it is highly likely your portfolio will outperform over time any investment offered by any broker or any actively managed mutual fund but virtually certain that it will outperform a selection of individual securities recommended by a broker.

Here is the security to buy for your initial portfolio: the Vanguard Total Stock Market Index Fund Investor Shares, symbol VTSMX. This fund holds, as of this date, shares in approximately 3,500 companies that mirror the entire market. To set up your account with Vanguard, call 1-877-662-7447 or visit www.vanguard.com. Remember your investment horizon is 50 years or more. Our security is tax efficient (i.e., it does not engage in trading practices that will cause taxable events that allow Uncle Sam to raid your portfolio periodically).

I have purposely chosen a single security so you will experience the daily fluctuations in the market value of your portfolio. You are, in effect, in training to experience market volatility. The market is going to reward you for taking the risk. You could have invested in a Certificate of Deposit at the bank and gotten a lower but secure return, but after accounting for inflation, you would have achieved a zero rate of return or possibly less. As of the date I write, the rate of return on a one-year CD is less than the rate of inflation. There is one problem with our plan. It is a very personal one and one that only you can handle. The worst enemy you will ever encounter in achieving your financial objectives is looking at you every morning in your mirror. Your success depends only on following the plan. Here is a little chart for you to fill out for the first year of the program. For the first year, I want you to invest 12% of your monthly earnings into your investment account. By way of example, if you earn $3,000 per month, invest $360 per month. I suggest you set this up with your bank so you won't forget. It will be painful for the first few months.

Month	Target Shares	Purchased Shares
1		
2		
3		
4		
5		
6		
7		
8		
9		
10		
11		
12		

Now for the chart. Go to your computer and find the current price for the security VTSMX or go to the newspaper to find symbol TotSt. Calculate the number of target shares you will be using to measure progress.. By way of example, divide the $360 by the price of the security and enter the target column for the first month; for the second month, your target is twice as many, and so forth until in the last row you have a number 12 times your first purchase. You must add the amount of $360 to you portfolio each and every month.

This is how we are going to evaluate your progress. We don't care what the value of the portfolio is or whether you have made or lost money. What we do care about is whether you are accumulating enough shares to retire in style. When stocks are cheap, we will be buying more shares, and when stocks are expensive, we will be acquiring fewer shares. This process is called dollar-cost averaging, and over time, as the market value of your stock increases, the average cost of the shares you have purchased will be less than their average price. This is accomplished by investing a fixed dollar amount monthly. With the fund we have selected, you pay no commission, and the expenses are currently two tenths of one percent yearly.

You must stick with your plan. Expect that the market value of the portfolio may vary as much as 30% from one year to another, and the temptation to bail out of the market will be strong. Believe me—I have been through it. If you have a portfolio worth $20,000 and the market punishes you with a 10% drop; that is a $2,000 decline in value. You are learning now how to survive these fluctuations without chickening out. Later, we will be adding securities representing different asset classes to increase portfolio return some of which will increase risk while other asset classes will decrease portfolio risk. To make it perfectly clear, I will complete the chart for you using a monthly addition of $360 per month when the stock is selling for $108.27 per share; 360/108.27=3.325 shares per month. This is how we are going to measure progress.

Month	Target Shares	Purchased Shares
1	3.325	
2	6.650	
3	9.975	
4	13.300	
5	16.625	
6	19.950	
7	23.275	
8	26.600	
9	29.925	
10	33.250	
11	36.575	
12	39.900	

For the second year, you will be adding two additional asset classes. The ones I like are small-cap stocks and a bond fund. Small-cap stocks are riskier investments than the total market index fund we started with. Stocks in this asset class will fluctuate by a wider range in price over the years. There will be long periods of time where small-cap stocks will underperform or outperform the total market for stocks. But the good thing is that the expected return will be higher.

For your small-cap portion of the portfolio, I have chosen the Vanguard Small-Cap Index Fund Investor Shares NAESX. We will allocate 10% of our funds from this point on to this asset class. This fund currently holds approximately 1,700 individual issues. What you are doing here is tilting your portfolio towards an asset class with higher returns, but with higher risk as well. As they say in securities there is no such thing as a free lunch. Securities with higher expected returns carry higher risk. The market insures that this occurs. It is the action of millions of investors that in the end that insures that there are no bargains in the market.

To control portfolio risk, we will add a bond fund. The Vanguard Total Bond Market Index Fund Investor Shares VBMFX fits the bill. This fund currently holds approximately 2,000 issues. To see all of the data on these funds and all of your holdings, go to www.vanguard.com and enter the stock symbols VTSMX, NAESX, and VBMFX.

The two stock funds, VTSMX and NAESX, we will call equities, and VBMFX is our fixed income fund. Our asset allocation is now VTSMX 70%, NAESX 10%, and VBMFX 20%

What we have now constructed is a portfolio of just three funds that have some very desirable characteristics, namely a portfolio that contains approximately 5,500 individual securities providing a degree of diversification not possible with either an actively managed mutual fund or by following broker recommendations. We have a portfolio that conforms to the characteristics of MPT. This portfolio has a higher risk adjusted return than each of the individual investments that make up the portfolio.

So here is your new chart to post results for your target for the second year. We are going to do this for your second year and then perform a procedure called rebalancing to gain additional returns. Post your accumulation of shares for the second and third years on the worksheets on the following page.

Month	Actual Shares VTSMX	Actual Shares NAESX	Actual Shares VBMFX
1			
2			
3			
4			
5			
6			
7			
8			
9			
10			
11			
12			
Month	**Actual Shares VTSMX**	**Actual Shares NAESX**	**Actual Shares VBMFX**
1			
2			
3			
4			
5			
6			
7			
8			
9			
10			
11			
12			

Once you get comfortable with the performance of your portfolio, then and only then may you add other asset classes for increased returns and reducing risks.

To mitigate the effects of inflation and provide additional diversification, we will add enough foreign securities to bring their weight in the equity portion of the portfolio to 30% (which is 24% of the total portfolio), To accomplish this, we will use the Vanguard Total International Stock Index Fund VGTSX. This fund holds approximately 1,700 securities in Europe and the Far East plus shares of companies in emerging countries. These additional asset classes will cause your portfolio to stray away from the performance of the U.S. market, sometimes for long periods of time, so be prepared to stay the course. Trust in time and you will do fine in the market. You are learning what risk is all about. This is a lesson you must learn to be successful in the stock market.

We now have approximately 6,500 securities in our portfolio. So here is what your portfolio will look like when fully funded.

- Total Stock Market Index Fund VTSMX 48%
- Small-Cap Index Fund NAESX 8%
- Total International VGTSX 24%
- Total Bond Market Index Fund VBMFX 20%

The ratio of equities to bonds is 80/20. As you age, you will decrease the equity portion and increase the fixed income portion of the portfolio.

It is unlikely that the asset classes in our portfolio will change at identical rates. To maintain the desired proportion of each asset class in the portfolio, you must periodically rebalance your account to the original allocation weights. This means you will be selling a portion of those asset classes that have done a great deal better than expected, thus skewing our original asset allocation, and adding more shares to the asset classes that have not done as well as planned. By way of example, over time, the equity asset classes will do much better than the fixed income asset class. By balancing the portfolio back to the original planned allocation, you are automatically buying low and selling high.

This procedure will, by the nature of the scheme, add approximately 0.5% to the expected return of the portfolio after taxes.

Of course, please use some judgment here and first add new money to the asset classes that need more stocks before you sell some of the winners. In selling a portion of the winners, you are incurring a tax liability for assets in a taxable portfolio. For those of you who have the subject assets in a tax-deferred portfolio, you will not have a taxable event when rebalancing. I would rebalance no more than once a year and only then when an asset class is about 5% or more out of balance. We like to say that the optimum portfolio violates all of the arithmetic theorems learned as a child because in a properly constructed portfolio, 2+2=5. Over time, the total return of the portfolio will exceed the weighted average of its parts provided we rebalance it back to the original asset allocations.

As the years roll forward, you will want to increase the allocation of fixed income securities from the now 80% in equities and 20% in debt securities (i.e., bonds) to a mix of 30% in equities and 70% in debt when you are in your early 70s. During retirement, you may be withdrawing from your portfolio amounts in excess of the portfolio income from interest earned and capital gains. Most advisors would recommend that your debt portion of your portfolio equal your age. An easy way of doing this is to divert enough funds monthly to keep your allocation of debt equal to your age.

For those of you that are in a 401(k) program, urge your employer to provide at least some index funds as a choice. If a total stock market fund is not offered, buy a fund that tracks the S&P 500, and for the other asset classes, buy those with the lowest expense ratios.

In financial jargon, you are an accumulating investor. During the accumulation phase, we are net buyers of securities; thus, we look favorably at lower prices. That means that the total value of our portfolio may, at times, decrease, perhaps even below our cost. It is vital that you continue your purchasing schedule during these times. The nice thing about a down market is that when you dollar-cost average into it, you are buying at lower prices and will recoup any unrealized losses faster when the market turns around. Your training in the first few years will, we hope, fortify your stamina for the down markets that you will surely experience a number of times in the future. Certainly, you should read the balance of the book, add to your investment library the other books I recommend, and go to the websites I recommend at your leisure, but do not get too aggressive in your investment program. Enjoy life, save your money, and follow this plan without fail. You are now in training to become a successful investor. If, however, you are inclined to be lazy and have neither the time nor inclination to learn how to invest, then I have another program for you that will provide good results with no effort on your part. This automatic investing program is discussed in the following section.

Automatic Portfolios

I offer two portfolios for the investor who does not want to be involved with actively managing their investments. The Star fund was highlighted on the cover of the book.

STAR Fund

You can invest in the Vanguard STAR Fund (VGSTX) for as little as $1,000 with monthly additions of as little as $100 or $50 with automatic bank withdrawals. This portfolio has domestic and foreign stock exposure and a variety of bonds at various maturities. **The fund has a current benchmark of 50% Dow Jones Wilshire 5000 Index, 25% Lehman Aggregate Bond Index, 12.5% Lehman 1–5 Year Credit Index, and 12.5% MSCI EAFE Index.**

The fund does not buy securities directly; instead, it invests in other Vanguard funds: eight equity funds and three bond funds. The fund, thus, gains exposure to stocks that vary widely by industry, by market capitalization, and by their growth or value orientation; to a diversified group of bonds; and to short-term investments. The fund allocates 60% to 70% of its assets to stocks, 20% to 30% to bonds, and 10% to 20% to short-term investments. The advantage for the small investor just starting out is immediate exposure to a diversified portfolio with a small $1,000 initial investment and monthly additions of $100 or more. In this manner, you can get started with an advanced portfolio well within your means. Investment in the STAR Fund requires no effort on your part—just leave it alone for 10 years or so; it will manage itself. In total, you will usually have in your portfolio over 2,500 securities professionally managed by some of the best managers in the business.

I choose to call the STAR Fund a hybrid fund. It follows an asset allocation policy suggested by a portfolio of index funds although actively managed fund expenses are kept at an absolute minimum. This fund has a benchmark comprised of indexes, but the asset allocation is not suggested by the indexes. Further, you have the advantage of having a piece of eight equity funds and three bond funds in your portfolio, covering a range of asset classes. For an initial $1,000 investment, you have the diversification equivalent to a portfolio with several thousand dollars invested.

Target Retirement Funds

There is another category of funds run by the Vanguard people worthy of consideration by those who want index fund exposure but do not want to bother with managing their portfolios. Some of the target retirement funds also invest in Vanguard Inflation-Protected Securities Fund, which is not an index fund.

The minimum initial investment is $1,000 with additions of $100 or more. These funds, a total of six in all, are selected by your age. These are Vanguard's Target Retirement Funds.

If you don't have the time, ability, or inclination to manage your retirement portfolio, then a Target Retirement Fund will do the work for you.

With target retirement funds, you have only one decision to make: when you plan to retire. Your target retirement fund automatically grows more conservative as your retirement age draws near. When you're ready to draw income in your retirement years, your target retirement fund has a stable, income-oriented mix of assets. You get it all in one low-cost fund—a fully diversified mix of stocks and bonds—

that's professionally managed for your stage of retirement planning.

Target retirement funds have different degrees of exposure to the stock and bond markets because each fund is subject to varying combinations of stock and bond market risks. For example, the Vanguard Target Retirement 2045 Fund has 89% of its assets in U.S. and international stocks and 11% in U.S. bonds. The high stock allocation means that the fund will initially have a lot of exposure to stock market risk, that is, a decline in market prices. In my opinion, should a general market decline occur, stocks are on sale and you will be buying at bargain prices as you add to your portfolio with monthly additions.

At the other end of the spectrum, Vanguard Target Retirement Income Fund VTINX has 75% of its assets in bonds 20% in stocks, and 5% in short-term reserves. The high allocation to bonds means that the fund would be highly influenced by bond market risks; however, the portfolio has a lesser degree of credit risk.

Symbol	**Age now**	**Years to retire**
VTIVX	20s	About 40
VTTHX	30s	About 30
VTTVX	40s	About 20
VTXVX	50s	About 10
VTOVX	60s	About 1–5
VTINX	Retired	Retired

Experienced Investors

If you are reading this book, you have, in all probability, been investing all wrong for a number of years. It is not shameful to admit that you have been a fool for so long. I know it was 20 years before I learned how to invest properly.

We are not going to waste our time and energy trying to select individual securities. Academia has proven that selecting individual stocks is a sub-optimum strategy.

Now, you are probably aware that the stock market goes up and down, and these fluctuations seem to occur at random. In fact, it appears to happen for no apparent reason. Rest assured that over the long run, the market appreciates at a rate of 7% to 9% per year. These are nominal numbers. From these numbers, you must subtract inflation to correct for purchasing power. This 7% to 9% rate of appreciation, or more correctly, total return, is tied to corporate earnings and dividend payments over the long term. We are not going to go into this subject in this book. Just accept the fact that over the long run, returns will be in the range of 7% to 9%. In the short run, market returns jump all over the map.

In the short run, that is, for periods as long as four years, the market for all stocks can go down as much as 50%. This is a normal, not unusual, event. There are ways to dampen the effect of these fluctuations on your portfolio. During the time you are an accumulating investor, you will be in a position to accept more risk than when you are cashing in your securities for your retirement years. For this period, we will use techniques to level out the fluctuations in the market value of your portfolio. We can reduce the volatility of your portfolio by adding asset classes with low coefficients of correlations to one another. Adding short-term bond funds accomplishes this objective. As you approach retirement age, your allocation to stocks will be reduced to 40% and the allocation to bonds will approach 60%. This is important because the majority of investors will be drawing down amounts in excess of the interest and dividends produced by the portfolio.

Some people will try to convince you that they can foresee downturns in the market, or bear markets, and can tell you when to sell to avoid losses and when to get back into the market when it is ready to go back up. Some of these fortunetellers work for major Wall Street brokerage firms. From personal experience, I can tell you that I have never known anyone who can tell you when the market will slide. Just remember: a market with lower prices means stocks are on sale. In the 1973 to 1974 time period, we had a huge sell off in over-the-counter stocks. By sheer luck, I made massive purchases of small company securities using all my credit resources. I borrowed on unsecured credit from the bank, refinanced the house, and deferred other purchases. Small company stocks were selling for their working capital and for as little as a price/earnings ratio (P/E) of 3X. As I write, the P/E for small-cap stocks is about 20X. A 20 P/E is an earnings yield of 5% (100/20=5%)—stock price divided by earnings per share or the price the public will pay for a dollar's worth of earnings. At a P/E of 20 times earnings, the public is paying $20.00 for each $1.00 of earnings.

During the early 1970s, you could buy a $1.00 of earnings for $3.00; thus, stocks today are about seven times as expensive. Does this mean that you should not buy stocks now? Not at all. It can be shown that the best strategy is to continue your accumulation plan. Attempting to invest when one thinks stocks are cheap and getting out of the market when stocks are expensive is called timing the market.

I want to keep you away from stockbrokers, financial planners, insurance salesmen, and other so-called "experts" who are compensated by selling you financial products of dubious value. To see the damage a full-service broker can do to your account, go to this website: http://www.efficientfrontier.com/ef/996/broker.htm.

We will be using Etrade as our discount broker. As described previously, this broker offers some of the lowest commissions available on the street and has a reputation for fair dealing with its customers. The fee for purchasing mutual funds and ETFs is $5.00 for up to 5,000 shares. Their margin rates are the most competitive on the street. We will not be using margins at this time but will have a margin account that allows us to have a ready cash reserve so to speak.

As I mentioned earlier, I want you to transfer any securities you own into an account with this broker because at the proper time, we will be liquidating single securities in favor of index funds. With single issues, you're taking on risks for which you are not receiving a proper expected return.

At this point, I urge you to read a paper by John Norstad titled *Investing in Total Markets*. It can be found at http://homepage.mac.com/j.norstad/finance/total.html. John is a regular contributor to a discussion forum held on the Morningstar website at http://socialize.morningstar.com.

It is on this website that you will find a continuous discussion by individual investors who follow passive investment strategies called the Diehards. These investors practice methods used by some of the largest pension plans and trusts. Diehards use index funds to form portfolios of equity and bond funds in such a manner as to obtain superior returns and reduce risk.

They follow methods set down by some of the finest minds in the academic community when it comes to investing in marketable securities. Diehards use index funds managed by The Vanguard Group, Inc., a unique organization in the financial services industry in that investors are charged only the cost of running Vanguard funds. To contact Vanguard, go to their website at www.vanguard.com.

Diehards use a forum sponsored by Morningstar. This forum has, since its inception, hosted some 350,000 conversations on approximately 40,000 topics. The forums receive some 25,000 hits daily. Once at the website, go to *Discuss,* then *Vanguard Diehards.* This is our forum.

Our mentor is John Bogle, the founder of the largest index fund in the world. The Vanguard Group manages over $800 billon in assets in a number of index funds and low-cost managed funds serving individual investors as well as the largest pension funds and trusts. We try to meet with Jack (he prefers Jack to John) at an annual get-together where some 100 Diehards meet to discuss their investments. Recently, local chapters have been formed where individual investors meet on an informal basis. Currently, there are 16 local chapters and another nine in the organizational phase. To locate a chapter near you, go to www.Lostsprings.com/diehards/chapters.

As of 2004, over $550 billion, one-sixth of equity fund assets, are indexed. There are now 430 equity index funds and 30 bond index funds. Your index fund tracks the entire U.S. stock market; other index funds track market segments such as the stocks of large companies, small companies, foreign securities, certain industry groups, retail, finance, health care, and so forth. Investors are thus able to purchase baskets of stocks and tilt their portfolios towards certain segments of the market. We will be tilting our portfolio toward small-cap companies and small and large-cap value stocks to obtain higher-than-total-market returns. We will also have a fixed income component to adjust the portfolio to the degree of risk we can tolerate at various stages of our investment life. For example, a young investor can afford to have a riskier portfolio while accumulating shares while an investor living off the income of his portfolio and selling off some of his shares every year needs insurance that within certain guidelines, he will not run out of money.

So now you are ready to buy your first security: the Exchange Traded Fund called the Vanguard Total Stock Market Viper (VTI)

Fund your account with the securities you transfer in or with cash to bring the balance to the minimum of $15,000. We will be adding money each month to the account automatically by means of a deduction from your bank account. Thus, you will be investing without even noticing the money going out.

Here is where we are now. You have purchased a diversified portfolio of 3,500 stocks and unlike actively managed mutual funds, there will be little or no trading that could generate taxable events in a taxable account; and, there is no "expert" skilled in convincing you to buy recommended stocks.

We are not going to trade; we are going to buy and hold what we bought, thereby avoiding a taxable event. We bought an ETF because the actions of other shareholders cannot cause a taxable event for your holdings. You will pay income taxes on the dividends received, however.

You should add a fixed amount of money to the account monthly; in this manner, when stocks are cheap you will accumulate more shares than when they are expensive. This is called dollar-cost averaging. The end result is that in the long run, the cost of the shares you accumulate will be less than the average market value of the shares.

Now we must figure out just how much we have to invest over the life of our income earning years to live a comfortable retirement. To do this, we will use a computer program at www.moneychimp.com. Go to this website and look for this form. Click on Calculator, then on Retirement. You will now see a form similar to the one below:

Inputs		
Current Principal	$	
Pre-Retirement		
Annual Addition	$	
Years to Grow		
Growth Rate		%
In Retirement		
Years to Pay Out		
Growth Rate		%
Results		
Annual Retirement Income	$	

Let's get started on figuring out how much we will put into our investment portfolio, how much it will earn, and what income you will enjoy during your retirement years.

By way of example, assume you are currently earning $50,000 per year and your spouse makes $35,000, so that is the income that you want to have at retirement date. You will need an income of $85,000 to retire comfortably. From the investments, you will receive $56,894.44 plus social security of say $2,500 per month or $30,000 for a total of $86,894.44 per year. You are 45 years old and have $35,000 saved, and together, you can put $10,200 a year towards your investments.

Fill in the boxes as follows:

- Current Principal $35,000
- Annual Addition (12% of $85,000) $10,200
- Years to grow (to age 65) 20 years
- Growth rate (used here 7.5%)
- Years to payout (used here life expectancy of age 85) 20 years
- Growth rate (used 7.5%)

Inputs	
Current Principal	$35,000
Pre-Retirement	
Annual Addition	$10,200
Years to Grow	20
Growth Rate	7.5%
In Retirement	
Years to Pay Out	20
Growth Rate	7.5%
Results	
Annual Retirement Income	$

Up to this point, you have a single security in your portfolio; now it is time to add additional asset classes. Some of the asset classes we will add are value stocks, small-cap stocks, and international securities. As we add these securities, our risk increases; it is axiomatic that asset classes with higher returns will carry additional risk. What we do is add an additional asset class with lower correlation. The asset class of choice is fixed income (i.e., short-term bonds).

Small company stocks are riskier than large-cap stocks and have higher returns. In fact, for the period 1927–2002, small-cap stocks returned annually 1.28% higher than large-cap stocks. Let's call this additional return the small-cap premium. The premium is related to the cost of capital for the small company. These companies must pay more for equity funds in the market place. Hence, they pay more for the costs of capital; the flip side of an increase in raising capital is the investor's additional return. By way of example only, an investment in Wal-Mart is a safer investment than, let's say, a single retail store in a small rural community or even a string of small stores in a number of rural towns.

Small-cap companies also pay more for borrowing from banks or even when issuing a bond. Their bond rating would not be as high as larger, established companies.

Another asset class is value companies. Be careful of the term value; Wall Street likes to latch onto catchy words. When we say "value stocks," we mean companies that are mature and not very exciting to own. They usually have slow growth and are unsure what will happen in the future for the business. They tend to pay out higher dividends. Often, value stocks are companies in financial distress.

Naturally, value stocks have higher rates of return. As an asset class, they have higher risk. People who establish indexes for small-cap and value stocks have special methods not of interest to us for identifying these companies. The value premium for large-cap stocks is about 3.3% higher than the market for a large-cap stock.

The premium for small-cap value stocks is approximately 4.0% higher than the market for small-cap stocks.

Here is our portfolio and the funds we will use for the equity portion.

- Vanguard Total Market Stock Vipers (Symbol VTI)—40% of the equity portion of the portfolio
- Vanguard Total Value Vipers (Symbol VTV)—10% of the equity portion of the portfolio
- Vanguard Small cap Vipers (Symbol VB)—10% of the equity portion of the portfolio
- Vanguard Small cap Value Vipers (Symbol VBR)—10% of the equity portion of the portfolio

For international exposure we use the following:

- Vanguard Emerging Market Stock Index Vipers (VWO)—10%
- Vanguard European Stock Index Vipers Index Fund (VKG)—10%
- Vanguard Pacific Stock Index Vipers (VPL)—10%

The international component adds to the diversification of the portfolio. To control the risk of the portfolio, that is, to make sure you don't chicken out in the face of a huge market sell off, we will add bonds to the asset mix. Adding an asset class that has low correlation with equities can control the volatility of the portfolio. So we use bonds.

We will add the Lehman 1–3 year Treasury Bond Index using iShares ETF (Symbol SHY).

The amount to add depends on your risk tolerance and your need for withdrawals from your portfolio during retirement. For the gung-ho investor, the very young, and those who have no choice, I would recommend an all-equity portfolio. By those with no choice, I mean those who have started too late in life to save for retirement. First to pay off credit card debt, then start to save with a vengeance. I recommend you buy and read a little book titled *The Richest Man in Babylon by George Clason.*

Now back to the risk adjustments. Many large pension funds use a 60/40 equity-to-debt ratio, and many individual investors use it as well.

As you age, you will be increasing the bond portion to even out the portfolio value each year. For the retired individual, a 30/70 equity-to-debt ratio is recommended.

If you cannot meet your retirement date objective, first try to invest more and then consider extending your retirement date a few years or increasing the risk in the portfolio by reducing the bond allocation or further increasing you small-cap allocation.

Please remember that the higher risk strategies recommended herein are as a whole far more conservative than investing in actively managed mutual funds.

Think about this. Only twice a year do you even know what you have invested in when you buy an actively managed mutual fund. We know fund managers are evaluated by comparing their results with the S&P index. We suspect that fund managers secretly invest in the index when their performance has suffered.

Dangerous Enemies to Avoid

This is an important section of the book. Everything you read here is supported by independent academic studies that have been peer reviewed or are from my fellow investors. There are four dangerous enemies of the individual investor. The enemies are brokers, the media (including TV), inflation, and taxes on investment income. We must avoid these sources of destruction to our savings plans and our portfolios at all costs. We are going to avoid these enemies or minimize their effects.

The financial press and the media are businesses, and they get their revenues from advertisements for which the sponsor pays. They are paid to develop interest in individual securities, which are coming to market or may come to the market in the near future. That is where the money is on Wall Street. Brokers sell stocks. With the right incentives, Wall Street brokers can sell anything and do.

These people are not investment experts; they are skilled salesmen who know little if anything about how to become successful as an investor. Simply stated, they may be required to extract 2% of your portfolio value in commissions each and every year. The average customer has an account valued at $75,000 from which the broker must obtain 2% one way or another; that's $1,500 per year. If, by some miracle, your account returned 9% over time with the advice of a full-service broker, the broker will have pocketed about 25% of the portfolio's return.

One of the best-kept secrets in the security industry is that security analysis-taken as whole-does not appear to be either useful or profitable.

What We Have Learned So Far

We have learned that stocks are risky investments, but we have also learned how to adjust the risk by adding fixed income assets to the portfolio. We have learned that stocks will fluctuate in value randomly, and no one can predict when that will happen. We have learned how to combine equities and bonds in such a manner as to reduce risk and increase return. Just how much increased return to expect will depend on how the market fluctuates over time, when you start your investment program, and the sequence and magnitude of stock price changes.

We are not going out to buy actively managed mutual funds; we know they underperform the market. We know that the fund manager is gambling with your money in hopes of looking good and earning a big bonus. Buying actively managed mutual funds is not a strategy. Even if successful in one year, there is no method to find an attractive fund that will outperform the market next year.

While we are on the subject of taxes, studies have shown, that taxpayers in the high tax brackets will, on average, surrender 55% of their accumulated portfolio wealth over time to Uncle Sam. Fortunately, taxpayers in the lower brackets loose only about 25% to the tax collector. These numbers are of total accumulated wealth in the portfolio. Not many investors are aware of the magnitude of money lost to taxes in actively managed mutual funds or broker-directed portfolios of individual securities, which pay the broker high commissions. At this point, I am going to recommend a book for you to read. Make a note of the title and author. Your entire investment library will consist of a dozen books or so by authors I believe are better than I am at explaining MPT.

W. Scott Simon titles the book *Index Mutual Funds*. It builds the case for passive investment strategies over and above using actively managed mutual funds and individual security selection better than any text I have read.

My book tells you how, and Simon's book tells you the why. You need the why data to help you brave the ups and downs of the market and fend off those who would convince you to participate in speculation. Wall Street has picked up on some of the nomenclature used by academia, mindful of the importance of MPT. As a result, they use the terms "allocation of assets in a portfolio" very loosely.

Let's look at the broad picture. You will see from time to time figures showing how a dollar or many dollars compound over the years to reach huge sums. What the writer left out is the little costs here and there that add up to large sums over time. The net return to investors is equal to the market return less the sum total of advisory fees, marketing expenditures, sales loads, brokerage commissions, transaction costs, custody and legal fees, and security processing costs.

Assume, then, that the market returns 10% annually and inflation takes away 3.5% as it has for as long as we have records; the real return becomes 6.5% or so. That is what we have after inflation is further reduced by another 4% due to intermediation costs and profits of active mutual funds. Subtract from the residual what your Uncle Sam takes by way of income taxes on dividends, interest, and capital gains; everyone makes money but you. The lesson learned here is that investment costs must be carefully managed. To do this, we all but eliminate transaction costs and commissions by reducing trading, which reduces taxes on capital gains; investing in low-cost index funds, which eliminates management costs for aggressively managed funds and their advertising and loads; and finally, making our own investment decisions. In a nutshell, there is basically no investment product that the individual investor should buy from a full-service brokerage house. There is no way that broker can hold his job without selling you stocks or funds that will extract 2% or more from portfolio. There is no reason to hire an investment advisor who provides free advice in exchange for selling you aggressively managed mutual funds that, on average, do not and cannot outperform the market.

Academic literature supports passive investment techniques. By passive, I mean buying a variety of index funds that buy broad groups of stocks of different asset classes and operate a buy-and-hold investment strategy. Brokers and actively managed mutual funds use their power of advertising and sales pitches to convince you that they can outperform the market. On a risk-adjusted basis, it is highly unlikely that they can outperform a market portfolio over time.

There are some excellent fee based Registered Investment Advisors that I know. Two of these gentlemen have written the books mentioned in the bibliography.

On the pages to follow please find some model portfolios constructed using modern portfolio theory. These portfolios are designed to have higher risk adjusted returns than each of the individual investments that make up the portfolio.

As a general rule the greater the uncertainty of the investment returns the higher the expected return. We deal with this uncertainty by adopting an investing strategy such as the one you have learned here. You are investing in risky investments because it is the only way to offset the damage that inflation can and will do to your savings. As you mature we will increase the allocation to fixed income securities.

Model Portfolios

The tables that follow show model portfolios for several investing situations.

High-income Portfolio

Total Stock Market	30%	VTSMX
High-yield Bond	10%	VWEHX
Total International	10%	VGTSX
Real Estate (REIT)	10%	VGSIX
Total Bond Market	40%	VBMFX

This portfolio is 50% equities and 50% fixed income if we count the real estate trust as an equity asset class security. I would rebalance the portfolio annually, first by adding new money to assets that have underperformed, then if necessary, selling off asset classes that have outperformed for the period. By rebalancing, you are automatically buying low and selling high. Over the next two decades, this portfolio should do as well as many portfolios with higher risks.

Do not expect this portfolio to follow one of the popular market indexes such as the S&P500 each and every year. At times it will fail to meet the S&P index. However the portfolio has lower risk or volatility. In later years a person near retirement years needs a portfolio with reduced risk. One does not want to be selling stocks when the market is going through one of its declining phases. Which I guarantee it will do from time to time.

Simple Three-fund Portfolio

Total Stock Market	35%	VTSMX
Total International Stock Index	15%	VGTSX
Total Bond Fund	50%	VBMFX

You heard it here. It is highly likely that this little three-fund portfolio will, over time, outperform any portfolio recommended by your full-service broker and all aggressively managed mutual funds as well on an after tax basis over the next twenty years with about one-third less risk. You will not experience periods of stress because it will track the popular stock market averages. The portfolio has several thousand equity stocks and several thousand fixed income securities.

The international component provides diversification as well as some hedge against the depreciation of the dollar. You may divide the international component into three asset classes if you like by substituting for the broad index Vanguard's Pacific Stock Index Fund (VPACX), Vanguard's European Index Fund (VEURX), and the Emerging Market FUND (VEIEX) in the ratios of 40/40/20

Caution: when you add these additional asset components, you increase the risk that your portfolio will not track the popular indexes such as the broad U.S. market indexes.

Slice & Dice Portfolio

Total Stock Market	10%	VTSMX
Large-cap Value	10%	VIVAX
Small-cap Index	10%	NAESX
Small-cap Value	10%	VISVX
Pacific	4%	VPACX
Europe	4%	VEURX
Emerging Markets	2%	VEURX
REIT	10%	VGSIX
Total Bond Market	40%	VBMFX

Slice & Dice refers to a discovery that a category of stocks called value stocks produce higher returns apparently at lower risk over time. Some say it is a free lunch so to speak; that is, you get a higher return without any additional risk. Others differ, saying there is additional risk.

By way of example, according to Jack Bogle "I'm not yet persuaded that "slice and dice" will improve "pure" bond/stock index returns. If "everyone" knows that value stocks will win, their prices will rise to reflect that expectation, arbitraging the past advantage away" we shall see...

We are not going to get into that argument, but we will develop a portfolio to the capture additional value returns should they continue to occur. This portfolio has a 60/40 equity-to-debt ratio very similar to that of large pension funds and trusts. There will be periods where this portfolio will not track popular indexes, so it is not for the faint of heart. Higher returns are always accompanied by higher risk. Sometimes, for many years, value stocks will stray from their long-term journey. Rest assured that over time they might outperform other asset classes and then go to sleep again. This is where your regular rebalancing practice comes into play. You sell securities that have outperformed their respective asset allocation and buy those that have underperformed. This periodic action results in increased returns for the investor. That's you my friend.

Conservative and More Aggressive Portfolios

The following portfolios have a 50% allocation to equities and a 50% allocation to debt securities and, therefore, are suitable to mid-life investors. Further, many students of the market have the opinion that equity and debt returns will be about equal over the next two decades. As a result, why take the risk of a higher allocation to equities when the return will approximate debt asset returns?

Conservative Portfolio*		
Stocks	50%	
Total Stock Market	20%	VTSMX
Small-cap Stocks	10%	NAESX
International Stocks	15%	VGTSX
REITs	5%	VGSIX
Bonds	50%	
Total Bond Market	30%	VBMFX
Short-term	10%	VBISX
Intermediate-term	10%	VBIIX

A More Aggressive Portfolio*		
Stocks	50%	
Large-cap Stocks	10%	VFINX
Small-cap Stocks	10%	NAESX
Large-cap Value Stocks	6%	VIVAX
Small-cap Value Stocks	6%	VISVX
International Stocks	6%	VGTSX
Emerging Markets	6%	VEIEX
REITs	6%	VGSIX
Bonds	50%	
Total Bond Market	20%	VBMFX
Short-term	20%	VBISX
Intermediate-term	10%	VBIIX

- Adapted from *Protecting Your Wealth in Good Times and Bad by Richard A. Ferri*

Extremely Aggressive Portfolios

The following portfolios are for the investor who has a lot of ground to make up and desires to build an aggressive portfolio to capture maximum returns from a portfolio of index funds.

This portfolio does not have a bond component so has about the same amount of risk as the average aggressively managed mutual fund, but has a greater likelihood of achieving the target returns. The objective of the portfolios is to achieve over time a return in the range of 2.5% to 3.0% over and above the market return currently estimated at 8.5% by some observers. An 11% total return over 30 years on $100,000 investment will yield approximately $2,289,000 before taxes on dividends and capital gains.

These portfolios are heavily tilted towards capturing both the small- cap stock and the value premium that have over the past 30 years has been shown to produce superior returns. There is no guarantee that the value premium will continue to persist. The market has a way of elimination such anomalies over time. You are gambling when you invest in an actively managed mutual fund but these portfolios may be a better bet. Time will tell. After taxes on capital gains I think this portfolio may be a better bet. Who knows?

DESCRIPT-IONS	SYM	ALLOC-ATION	EXPENSE RATIO	# STOCKS
LG-CAP MARKET	VV	30%	0.11%	426
LG-CAP VALUE	VTV	30%	0.11%	403
SM-CAP MARKET	VB	20%	0.12%	997
SM-CAP VALUE	VBR	20%	0.12%	957

The all Vanguard portfolio has a slight edge in that it has lower expense ratios, but the disadvantage that it may not be as good in capturing the small-cap premium. I have no preference for one portfolio over the other. When you invest in either of these portfolios you must be patient. There will be periods of time when they will under perform the market for extended periods of time. The value premium appears to be without additional risk. There may be a risk factor in the value premium we cannot see.

When this portfolio falls behind keep adding to the portfolio. In this manner when the portfolio does well you will recover lost ground more rapidly than if you exited the market for a period of time.

Using Russell ETF's and the new Micro-Cap ETF

DESCRPT-IONS	SYM	ALLOC-ATION	EXPENSE RATIO	INDEX
LG-CAP MARKET	IWB	30%	0.15%	RUSSELL 1000
LG-CAP VALUE	IWD	30%	0.20%	RUSSELL LG-CAP 1000
MICRO-CAP **	IWC	20%	0.60%	2,000**
SM-CAP VALUE	IWN	20%	0.25%	RUSSELL SM-CAP VALUE

.

** New micro-cap index fund designed to capture the micro-cap premium, contains 2,000 issues. These portfolios are designed to obtain the maximum returns available without gambling on individual stock selection.

Investors are advised that these portfolios are only for those who can stomach portfolio values taking on radical volatility characteristics. Further the value premium is not at all a permanent fixture. The market may very well erase its premium over time as the market has on, any other anomalies. These portfolios will stray from the popular indexes on occasion and sometimes for many years. They have done so in the past and will do so in the future. To capture the potential of these portfolios one must re-balance the portfolios periodically.

Conclusion

I have supplied you with the essential information to build an optimum portfolio of marketable securities that will appreciate over time to a value sufficient to live out your retirement years is style and comfort. By now, you should have been convinced that passive investment techniques are the only method by which you have any reasonable chance of reaching your goals. If you are not convinced, then I will ask you to read the books I have recommended in the appendix until you come to the conclusion that the method and strategy promoted here is the only way one can achieve success with any degree of confidence.

There is no other strategy that has proven to be successful. There is no method ever proposed that has ever shown to be capable of achieving greater-than-market returns. There is no analyst, broker, brokerage firm, or consultant who can show you a record of successes that have been achieved except those few that have been lucky. Yes, I will admit that there are a number of individual investors who have shown extraordinary skill in selecting individual stocks. Of those few exceptions, none has ever been identified in advance of the accomplishment. We have never been able to rule out that their accomplishment has been due to skill or just plain luck. Can one select an aggressively managed mutual fund that will outperform the market? The answer is no, one cannot do so.

Select a portfolio of index funds in accordance with the guidelines set forth in this book. A market equity fund matched with a bond fund in the ratio of 60% equities and 40% bonds is a respectable portfolio that will produce a return that will over time outperform any portfolio of stocks suggested by any broker, consultant, or any other so-called expert you will ever come across. Of this I am certain and have tons of careful studies to prove the assertion.

Now comes the hard part. We can expect that from time to time, the market will react to unknown conditions and bid up the prices of securities to values far in excess of their average, and at other times, prices will decline below the average trend. There is no known method to determine these occurrences before they occur or even know at what stage the speculation may level off or decline.

Because of the volatility in market prices, you will feel as if you are throwing money away when you make your monthly additions to your portfolio. Trust me, during these periods; stocks are on sale and being offered at bargain prices. Here is where the average investor and even those who have been investing for many years may need help. I have suggested that you look at you stock holdings by measuring your progress on number of shares of the funds that you are accumulating not their market value. By systematically adding to your portfolio every month in times of market decline, you will be accumulating additional shares, shares over and above your original plan, Further, when the portfolio gets out of balance (i.e., the proportion of the equities exceeds that of your allocation), bring the portfolio back into the original plan by selling equities. You are then selling at market highs. The reverse is true when the market value of your equities causes your allocation of equities to go below the plan; you will be buying equities to rebalance your portfolio or buying low.

These are times that cause the majority of investors' pain and suffering. Even the most devout fan of passive investing techniques will find their resolve questioned. You will be tempted to reduce exposure to equities just at the time when you should be purchasing additional shares. If you yield to the temptation, you will be selling at market lows. Those who study investor patterns can see this very clearly in the data.

Experienced investors agree that one cannot successfully time the market in order to profit by purchasing stocks before they increase in price or sell securities just prior to when they are going to decline. **Take my word on this; do not try to disprove it by wasting your savings in a futile effort to profit by market movements.**

I have a solution for those periods when you are tempted to abandon the carefully developed investment plan you have selected. Just log onto the Morningstar website and post your feelings. You will immediately get help from those who have weathered a similar situation in the past and have been helped through the period by their peers. The ability to communicate with other investors and get help is crucial to your success.

During your investment career, it is highly likely that you will be approached many times by those who seek to convince you that they can select stocks that will produce extraordinary returns. Don't fall for these schemes. Worse, you may be approached by someone who wants to sell you a system that will find stocks poised to make large and profitable gains on the basis of a computer system that has verified its method. A typical characteristic of such schemes is that the system has screened 15 years of data using 50 or so parameters and has selected the few winners from the data. Salesmen who pitch these schemes really believe in the systems they are selling. Several thousand dollars is the average price of such programs. Any one who has a background in statistics knows that the more parameters you screen, the more likely you are to find a few securities that have historically produced great returns in the past and are just as unlikely to repeat the performance in the future.

I have presented you with a number of model portfolios, a few very conservative ones and some that have more risk but offer higher potential expected returns. It is more important to pick one of these portfolios and stick to its allocation than trying to find the best one. Make your selection and estimate your risk tolerance then go on the Diehard website and show your portfolio to the group. You will receive expert advice about your decision.

There is no correct portfolio, and in fact, it is more important to stick with your allocation plan. For those who do not want to get involved with annual rebalancing, just select one of the automatic portfolios and take a look at your portfolio every couple of years or so and adjust your additions accordingly.

Good luck. Yes, a degree of luck always helps. Investing is not an exact science, but what I have shown you are as close as you will ever find.

You can order additional copies of this book directly from the author by sending $8.00 in cash to Gordon L. Eade at 2941 Simitan Dr. Lake Havasu City, Arizona 86404. Each copy will be autographed by the author. From time the book will be updated to contain current information and new developments.

If you are ordering for your children or grandchildren I offer a special price of $5.00 for each book, minimum order at this price is four books. They will be shipped at the book rate to one address only.

Attention employers with 401k plans for your employees. Many plan sponsors do not provide access to no load index funds- this is a big mistake. You can do your employees a favor by transfer your 401k plan to Vanguard. Then provide your employees a copy of this book for their use. For bulk orders of 100 books or more the price is $3.00 per book. Send your business check to the address above.

From time to time check in to the author's web site for up to date information and corrections to this book. The address is www.index101.net

Appendix

Books to Read

The Bogleheads' Guide to Investing by Taylor Larimore, Mel Lindauer, and Michael LeBoeuf

Common Sense on Mutual Funds by John C._Bogle

All About Asset Allocation by Richard A, Ferri

*All About Index Funds*_by Richard A. Ferri

Protecting Your Wealth in Good Times and Bad by Richard A. Ferri

The Intelligent Asset Allocator by William Bernstein

Index Mutual Funds by W.Scott Simon

Rational Investing in Irrational Times by Larry E. Swedroe

Winning the Loser's Game by Charles D. Ellis

The Exchange Traded Funds Manual by Gary I. Gastineau

The Informed Investor by Frank Armstrong III

A Random Walk Down Wall Street by Burton G. Malkiel

Winning Investment Strategy by Larry E. Swedroe

Exchange Traded Funds by Jim Wiandt & Will McClatchy

The Four Pillars of Investing by William Bernstein

Websites

www.Morningstar.com

On this website, you will find conversations among investors who follow the strategies I recommend. Go to the box titled Discuss and click on Diehards. There are about 375,000 postings in these conversations.

www.moneychimp.com

On this website, you will find a wealth of information from portfolio theory to sophisticated computer simulations to discover within limits how long your retirement savings will last.

www.vanguard.com

This is the official website for the Vanguard Group. Here you can find detailed descriptions and up to date data on every Vanguard Index Fund as well as their actively managed Mutual Funds.

http://www.altruistfa.com/readingroomarticles.htm

At this website you will find hundreds of articles on finance and investments that are of interest to those who wish to fine tune their portfolios and keep abreast of developments.

www.Lostsprings.com/diehards/chapters.

At this web site you will find the location and schedule of a group of investors who follow passive investing techniques using Vanguard low cost index funds. These investors meet periodically at local chapters throughout the country. At these meetings you will meet other investors eager to help you with your investment program and to supply you with support during those uncomfortable periods when the market crashes for no reason at all, which it will surely do a couple times during your accumulation phase.